Prophet ﷺ Muhammad

Where the Story Begins

Farhana Islam

Illustrator **Eman Salem**

Chapter 1 – Amina and Abdullah

Our story begins long, long ago in the beautiful city of Makkah.

It was there a powerful chief lived with his young daughter,
Amina bint Wahb. Soon, she would marry the son of another
great chief, a young man named Abdullah ibn Abd al-Muttalib.
It didn't take long for the people of Makkah to find out about
their engagement, and when their marriage was announced,
everybody celebrated.

Not long after they married, Abdullah left Makkah to travel far away to a place called Sham (Syria). The journey was long and exhausting, it would take weeks upon weeks to ride all the way to Sham and back on a camel. This brought tears to Amina's eyes. Abdullah's father, Abd al-Muttalib was just as dismayed to hear of Abdullah's journey. Although he had many sons, Abdullah always had a special place in his father's heart.

But sadly, Abdullah needed to leave.

Weeks went by and Abdullah had yet to return home to Amina and his father. News eventually reached them that Abdullah had fallen gravely ill on his journey back home. Not long after, Abdullah passed away in the city of Yathrib (Madinah), never learning that he would soon become a father. Amina's heart had broken, as had Abd al-Muttalib's, knowing this child would be without a father.

Months passed and Amina prepared for the birth of her child. News later spread that she had been blessed with a beautiful, baby boy whom she named Ahmad.

Abd al-Muttalib was so overjoyed with the birth of his grandson that he also gave his new grandson a name of his own.

It was a name no one had heard of before.

It was a name that would carry generations of Muslims for many, many years to come.

That name was Muhammad ﷺ.

Chapter 2 – Halimah Sa'diyyah

Not long after the birth of Muhammad ﷺ, a kind-hearted woman by the name of Halimah Sa'diyyah was travelling across the Arabian desert with her tribe. They were on their way to Makkah, desperately in search of paid work.

It was not unusual for families to send their newborn children to live in the desert; often with women like Halimah, so their children would grow to become healthy, strong and eloquent in speech. This was Halimah's job and she very much loved her job. She would feed, clothe, bathe, and love these children as if they were her own.

Unlike those she travelled with, Halimah only had a frail, old camel and a worn-out donkey to call her own. Together they struggled to keep up with the rest of the travellers as Halimah's long journey continued across the sandy landscape and cloudless sky.

But still, she strived.

Still, she continued.

By the time they reached the city of Makkah, all of the children had been taken.

All but one.

Fortunately for Halimah, that child was the son of Amina bint Wahb and the grandson of Abd al-Muttalib.

That child was Muhammad ﷺ.

Little did she know that Allah had planned for this.

Little did she know that Allah would shower her and Muhammad ﷺ with blessings upon blessings.

Instantly, Halimah felt a powerful bond with Muhammad ﷺ and she knew she had to care for this child. In that moment, Halimah's donkey and camel grew in strength. In that moment she knew all that she needed to know.

Muhammad ﷺ was destined for great things.

Chapter 3 – The Angel Jibreel

Two years had passed and Halimah and her tribe were preparing to return the children to their families in the city of Makkah. Halimah loved Muhammad ﷺ more than she had loved any child. She wept and she wept. She would miss him dearly. And when the time came and Muhammad ﷺ was reunited with his loving mother Amina, Halimah begged to care for him a little while longer.

It was not an easy decision. It took some time, Amina loved her child, she missed him deeply and did not want him to leave once more. Eventually, by the will of Allah, Amina agreed and off Muhammad ﷺ went to live a peaceful life with Halimah and her family.

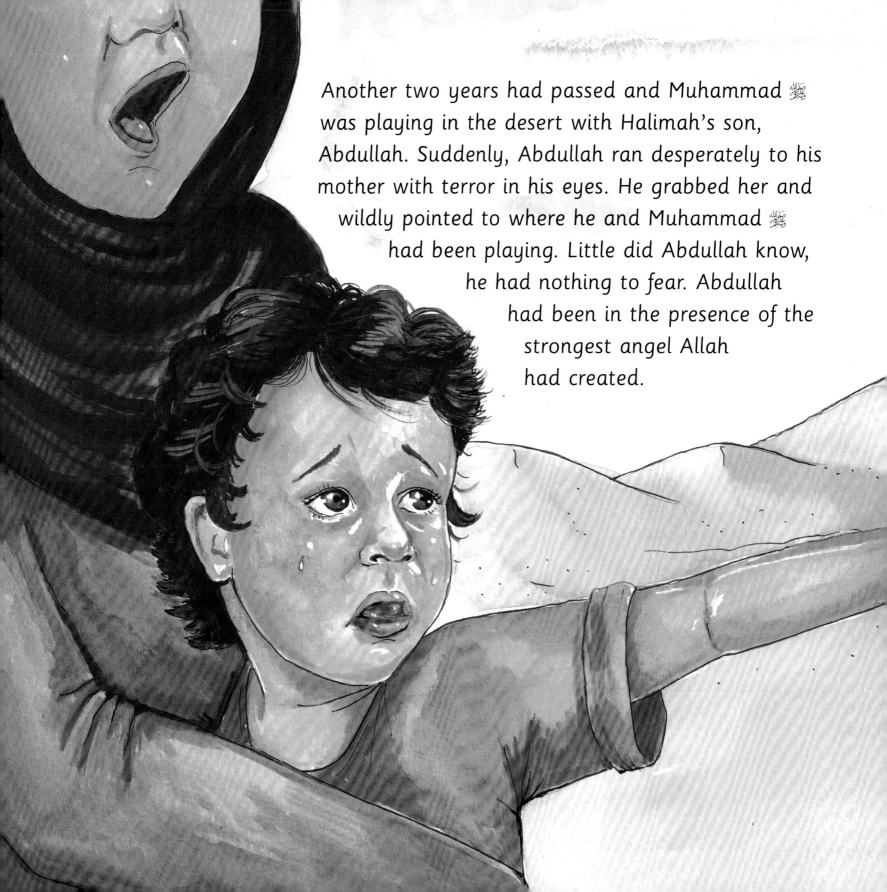

Another two years had passed and Muhammad ﷺ was playing in the desert with Halimah's son, Abdullah. Suddenly, Abdullah ran desperately to his mother with terror in his eyes. He grabbed her and wildly pointed to where he and Muhammad ﷺ had been playing. Little did Abdullah know, he had nothing to fear. Abdullah had been in the presence of the strongest angel Allah had created.

The angel Jibreel appeared in front of Muhammad ﷺ but unlike the other children, Muhammad ﷺ showed no fear. Suddenly, angel Jibreel did something no human would ever be able to do. With his bare hands, he reached out at Muhammad ﷺ and clutched at his heart. Angel Jibreel did something unheard of. He cleaned Muhammad's ﷺ heart with the purest, freshest water there is to exist.

He purified Muhammad's ﷺ heart with zam zam water.

This frightened Halimah and her family a great deal. They couldn't understand why somebody would do such an upsetting thing to a special child like Muhammad ﷺ. They didn't know what to believe or who to tell. In that moment Halimah and her family made a difficult decision.

They decided to take Muhammad ﷺ back to the city to be with his mother, Amina. Not because they did not want Muhammad ﷺ anymore, but because they loved him so much, they would rather be without him than see any harm come to him.

Halimah and her family had no idea that this would be the first of many encounters Muhammad ﷺ would have with the angel Jibreel.

Chapter 4 – The City of Yathrib

It was as if Allah had answered Amina's prayers. She was delighted to have Muhammad ﷺ home and she had complete faith that nothing would bring him harm.

For a long time, they lived happily and peacefully. Everybody cared a great deal for Muhammad ﷺ as he was the son of Abdullah and the grandson of the great, respected chief, Abd al-Muttalib.

After some time, Amina thought long and hard and decided to visit the beautiful city of Yathrib (Madinah). Despite her husband and Muhammad's ﷺ father, Abdullah, being buried there many years ago, Amina had never been.

So, she prepared her camels and was joined by Muhammad ﷺ and a woman named Barakah. Barakah was a blessed, gentle woman who showed nothing but love for Amina and Muhammad ﷺ for many, many years. Together, they waved goodbye to Abd al-Muttalib and began their long, tiring journey to the city of Yathrib.

The journey was difficult, but by the will of Allah, they made it there safely. Muhammad ﷺ spent time with Barakah as Amina visited Abdullah's grave.

And it wasn't long before they were on the road again heading back to Makkah. This time the journey was even more difficult. Nobody but Allah knew that this journey would be Amina's last. Just like Abdullah, Amina had fallen gravely ill on the journey back home. Amina knew her fate.